ANTARCTICA

by Claire Vanden Branden

Cody Koala

An Imprint of Pop!
popbooksonline.com

abdobooks.com
Published by Pop!, a division of ABDO, PO Box 398166, Minneapolis, Minnesota 55439. Copyright © 2019 by POP, LLC. International copyrights reserved in all countries. No part of this book may be reproduced in any form without written permission from the publisher. Pop!™ is a trademark and logo of POP, LLC.

Printed in the United States of America, North Mankato, Minnesota.

082018
012019

THIS BOOK CONTAINS
RECYCLED MATERIALS

Cover Photo: iStockphoto
Interior Photos: iStockphoto, 1; Shutterstock Images, 5 (top), 5 (bottom left), 5 (bottom right), 6, 9, 10, 13 (top), 13 (bottom left), 13 (bottom right), 14, 17, 19; Yonhap/AP Images, 20

Editor: Charly Haley
Series Designer: Laura Mitchell

Library of Congress Control Number: 2018949235
Publisher's Cataloging-in-Publication Data
Names: Vanden Branden, Claire, author.
Title: Antarctica / by Claire Vanden Branden.
Description: Minneapolis, Minnesota: Pop!, 2019 | Series: Continents | Includes online resources and index.
Identifiers: ISBN 9781532161704 (lib. bdg.) | ISBN 9781641855419 (pbk) | ISBN 9781532162763 (ebook)
Subjects: LCSH: Antarctica--Juvenile literature. | Continents--Juvenile literature. | Geography--Juvenile literature.
Classification: DDC 919.89--dc23

Hello! My name is

Cody Koala

Pop open this book and you'll find QR codes like this one, loaded with information, so you can learn even more!

Scan this code* and others like it while you read, or visit the website below to make this book pop.

popbooksonline.com/antarctica

*Scanning QR codes requires a web-enabled smart device with a QR code reader app and a camera.

Table of Contents

Chapter 1

Antarctica

Antarctica is farther south than any other **continent**. On a map, it looks like Antarctica is on the bottom of the world.

Watch a video here!

MAP OF ANTARCTICA

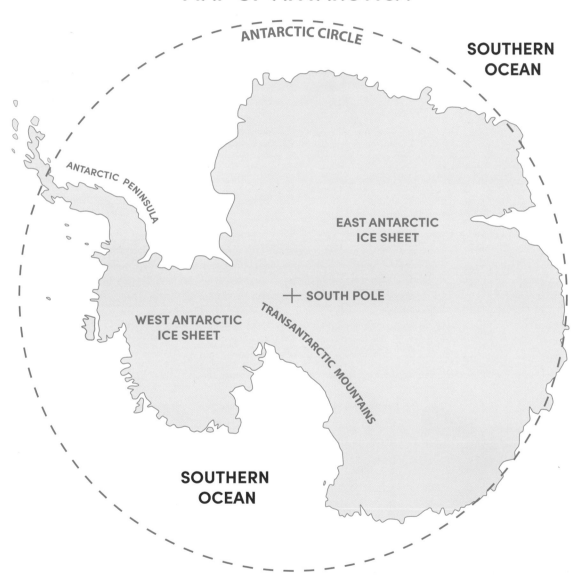

ANTARCTIC CIRCLE

SOUTHERN OCEAN

ANTARCTIC PENINSULA

EAST ANTARCTIC ICE SHEET

+ SOUTH POLE

WEST ANTARCTIC ICE SHEET

TRANSANTARCTIC MOUNTAINS

SOUTHERN OCEAN

There are no countries in Antarctica. Most of the continent is made up of the Antarctic ice sheet. This is the largest piece of ice in the world.

Antarctica was the last continent found by people. It was **discovered** in 1838.

Chapter 2

Cold and Windy

Antarctica is the coldest place on Earth. It does not snow very often there. When it does snow, the snow stays on the ground for many years.

Learn more here!

The South Pole is in Antarctica. It is the farthest south of any point on Earth. Antarctica has many mountains. There are also more than 90 volcanoes!

Antarctica is the windiest place on Earth.

Chapter 3

Animals and Plants

Many animals call Antarctica home. Many spend time in water and on land. The water feels warmer to animals like the emperor penguin.

Learn more here!

Many kinds of seals and whales live in Antarctica too. The leopard seal and the orca whale both hunt in the icy waters. They eat fish and other animals.

There are no trees in Antarctica because the **climate** is so cold. Most of the plants that grow are moss or algae.

Chapter 4

People of Antarctica

There are no people **native** to Antarctica. However, many **researchers** live there. They visit for months at a time to study the environment.

Complete an activity here!

The ice in Antarctica is melting. It would be bad for Earth if the ice melts completely. Scientists study Antarctica to help stop this from happening.

Making Connections

Text-to-Self

How is Antarctica different from where you live?
How is it the same?

Text-to-Text

Have you read another book about Antarctica?
What did you learn?

Text-to-World

Researchers live in Antarctica year-round. Why do
you think it is important that scientists study the
frozen continent?

Glossary

climate – the typical weather of a place or area over time.

continent – one of the seven large land masses on Earth.

discover – to find out about something.

native born in a certain place.

researcher – a person such as a scientist who studies and learns about a subject.

Index

Online Resources

popbooksonline.com

Thanks for reading this Cody Koala book!

Scan this code* and others like it in this book, or visit the website below to make this book pop!

popbooksonline.com/antarctica

*Scanning QR codes requires a web-enabled smart device with a QR code reader app and a camera.